Born Is the King

A Christmas Musical for the Senior Choir

Written and Arranged by

MARTY PARKS

lillenas.com

CONTENTS

The First Noel

Traditional English Carol
and KEN BIBLE

W. Sandys' *Christmas Carols*
Arranged by Marty Parks

el the an - gel did say Was to
13
13
cer - tain poor shep - herds in fields as they
lay–
17
17
In fields where they lay
In fields where they

21
keep - ing their sheep On a cold win - ter's
lay keep - ing sheep, Cold win - ter's
21
CD: 2
night that was so deep.
night that was so deep.
26
Divisi
No - el, No - el, No -
Divisi
26

(,)
30
el, No - el!
Born is the
(,)
30
King of Is - ra - el!
CD: 3
34
Ladies unison
mf
Then

37
Divisi
by the light of a bril - liant
mf
star, Three wise men came from
41
coun - try far.
45
They hum - bly
Unison mf
45

bowed and wor - shipped there, With
49
CD: 4
gold and myrrh and in - cense
rare.
f
54
No - el, No -
Divisi
f

(,)
el, No - el, No - el!
(,)
58
Born is the King of Is - ra -
58
el!
62
CD: 5
62

Unison
66
Now let us
Unison
66

Divisi
all with one ac - cord Sing
Divisi

70
prais - es to our Heav - en - ly
70

Unison
74
Divisi
Lord; With shep - herds, kings and
Unison
Divisi
74
an - gels come And wor - ship
78
78
CD: 6
Christ, the Ho - ly One!

Optional descant (solo or small group)
83
f
No - el, No -
No - el, No - el,
83
el, No - el, No - el!
(,)
No - el, No - el!
(,)

87
Born is the King of Is - ra -
87
el!
91
ff
He is born,
ff
91
ff
Born is the King!
8vb

NARRATOR: This is the way it happened–the birth of this King we sing about. The emperor, Caesar Augustus, had issued a royal decree that everyone under Roman authority should be counted. As each went to his own hometown, Joseph left Nazareth and began the journey to Bethlehem because he was a descendant of King David. He had already been told by an angel that Mary, who would soon be his wife, was expecting a child conceived by the Holy Spirit.

And so, with Mary, he approached Bethlehem just as the time came for the baby to be born. Mary gave birth to her firstborn child, a son. There was no place in any of the inns for this new family and so they had to make do with what they could find. Mary wrapped her new baby not in royal robes, but in swaddling clothes. She placed him, not on a throne as befits a king, but in a manger.

Once in Royal David's City

CECIL FRANCIS ALEXANDER

MARTY PARKS
Arranged by Marty Parks

11

Where a moth - er laid her Ba - by In a man - ger

11

for His bed.

15 *Divisi*

Mar - y was that moth - er mild–

Divisi

15

CD: 8

Je - sus Christ, her lit - tle Child.

*This verse may be performed entirely as one solo.

CD: 10
Sav - ior ho - ly.
35
Choir
f
Unison
And our eyes at last shall see Him Thro' His own re -
Unison f
35
f
39
Divisi
deem - ing love; For that Child so dear and gen - tle
39

Unison
43
Divisi
Is our Lord in heav'n a - bove. And He leads His
Divisi
43
chil - dren on To the place where He is
47
gone.
47
decresc.
rit.
mp

NARRATOR: *(music begins)* There were some shepherds nearby in the fields of Bethlehem. They were tending their flocks that night when suddenly an angel of the Lord appeared to them, shining with heaven's glory. "Don't be afraid," the angel said. "I have the most astounding news! A Savior has been born to you; He is Christ the Lord. He is in Bethlehem and this will be your sign: He's wrapped in cloths and lying in a manger."

Then with the angel there appeared a large number of heaven's host. They all praised God and said, "Glory to God in the highest, and peace on earth!"

Worship the King

Traditional English Carol, alt.

W. Sandys' *Christmas Carols*
Arranged by Marty Parks

18

Divisi

el, No - el, No - el, No - el!

Divisi

18

mp

22

Born is the King, Joy - ful - ly sing, And

22

26

wor - ship the King of Is - ra - el!

26

When Christ Was Born on Earth

Ladies Choir

English Text by JOE E. PARKS

Italian Carol
Arranged by Marty Parks

(11)

night, Like noon - day sun there

CD: 14

shone from the heav - ens a glo - ry won - drous

bright. *Divisi* *mf* Ra - diant - ly (15) shin - ing, Je - sus en -

shrin - ing, o - ver the vil - lage of Beth - le -

19
hem; To show the Sav - ior's birth, God
sent a light that shone down so bright - ly when
23
CD: 15
Christ was born on earth.
28
A - bove the sta - ble

small the glo - ry shone a - round; While
32
CD: 16
an - gels sang to shep - herds the mes - sage of
God Him - self come down. Ra - diant - ly
36
shin - ing, Je - sus en -
shrin - ing, o - ver the vil - lage of Beth - le - hem; To

40
show the Sav - ior's birth,
God sent a light that
shone down so bright - ly when Christ
44
was born on
earth.
When Christ was
48
born on earth.

As Lately We Watched

Men's Choir

Traditional

Austrian Carol
Arranged by Marty Parks

18
Divisi
light; All thro' the night an - gels did
22
sing Sweet car - ols in praise of the birth of a
26
CD: 19
Solo
mf
King! A
29
King of such beau - ty was ne'er be - fore seen, And
mf

33
Mar - y, His moth - er, so like to a queen.
37
Blest be the hour, wel - come the morn; For
41
CD: 20
Christ, our dear Sav - ior, on earth now is born.
Men unison
f
Then
46
shep - herds be joy - ful and hon - or your
f

CD: 21
50
King; Let hills ring and dales to the song that ye
54
Divisi
sing. Blest be the hour, wel - come the
58
morn; For Christ, our dear Sav - ior, on earth now is
62
born. For Christ, our dear Sav - ior, on

66

earth now is born.

66

He is born! He is

70

born!

70

Ped. *

NARRATOR: Just for a moment, let's pause and reflect on this wonderful Christmas story. Christ, the King of heaven, became a tiny child, born in humble surroundings and noticed by only a few. Yet, the response of the shepherds can be ours as well. For to us is born a Savior. *(music begins)* Let's kneel before Him in worship and adoration.

Let Us Adore Him

Words and Music by
MARTY PARKS
Arranged by Marty Parks

CD: 23
dore Him, The Sav - ior of us all.
Unison mf
14
O hear the an - gels sing,
Unison mf
Hear the an - gels
14
mf
"Glo - ry to our King!"
sing to our King!
18
And kneel be - fore His
18

(22) *Divisi*

maj - es - ty. O come, let us a -

Divisi

(22)

dore Him, Christ, the

(26) CD: 24 *Unison* ***f***

Lord. O

Unison ***f***

(26)

cresc.

f

30
come, let us a - dore Him, King of Heav - en
30
34
Divisi
Lord of all; O come, let us a - dore Him, The
Divisi
34
CD: 25
Unison
Sav - ior of us all.
O

(39)

hear the an - gels sing, "Glo - ry to our___

Unison

Hear the an - gels sing to our

(39)

(43)

King!" And kneel be - fore His maj - es - ty.

King!

(43)

(47) *Divisi*

O come, let us a - dore___ Him,

Divisi

(47)

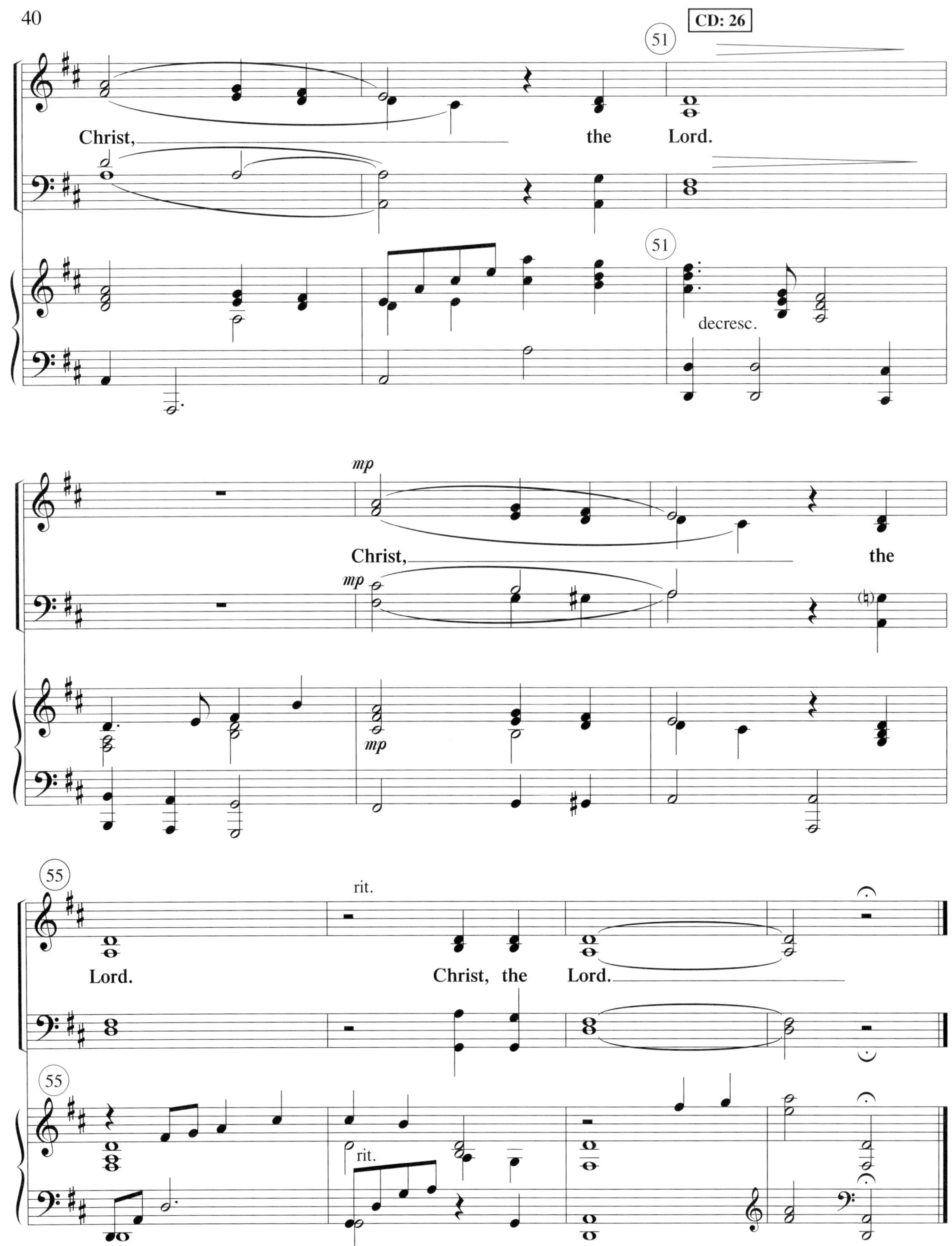
CD: 26
51
Christ, the Lord.
51
decresc.
mp
Christ, the
mp
mp
55
rit.
Lord.
Christ, the Lord.
55
rit.

Hark! the Herald Angels Sing

CHARLES WESLEY

MARTY PARKS
Arranged by Marty Parks

CD: 28

10
Peace on earth, and mercy mild–
God and sinners reconciled."
14 Divisi
Joyful, all ye
nations, rise;
Join the triumph of the skies.

18
With th'an - gel - ic host pro - claim,
18
CD: 29
"Christ is born in Beth - le - hem."
24
Unison
Hark! the her - ald an - gels sing,
Unison
24

CD: 30

Divisi
"Glo - ry to the new - born King."
Divisi
30
Unison
Hail, the heav'n - born Prince of Peace!
30
34
Light and life to
Hail, the Sun of Righ - teous - ness!
Unison
34

CD: 31
all He brings,
Ris'n with heal - ing in His wings.
38
Divisi
Mild He lays His glo - ry by, Born that man no
Divisi
38
more may die, Born to raise the sons of earth,
42
42

CD: 32
Born to give them sec - ond birth.
48
Unison
Hark! the her - ald an - gels sing,
Unison
48
Divisi
"Glo - ry to the new - born King."
Divisi

54

Unison

Glo - ry to, ___

Glo - ry to, ___

Unison

54

58

Glo - ry to ___ the new - born King!

58

Divisi

The new - born King!

Divisi

He Is the King

Traditional English Carol, alt.

W. SANDYS' *Christmas Carols*
Arranged by Marty Parks

NARRATOR: Angels proclaimed it, Shepherds responded to it. And later Wise men from the east acknowledged it. A King has been born! The Lord has come. Praise and glory to the King of kings.

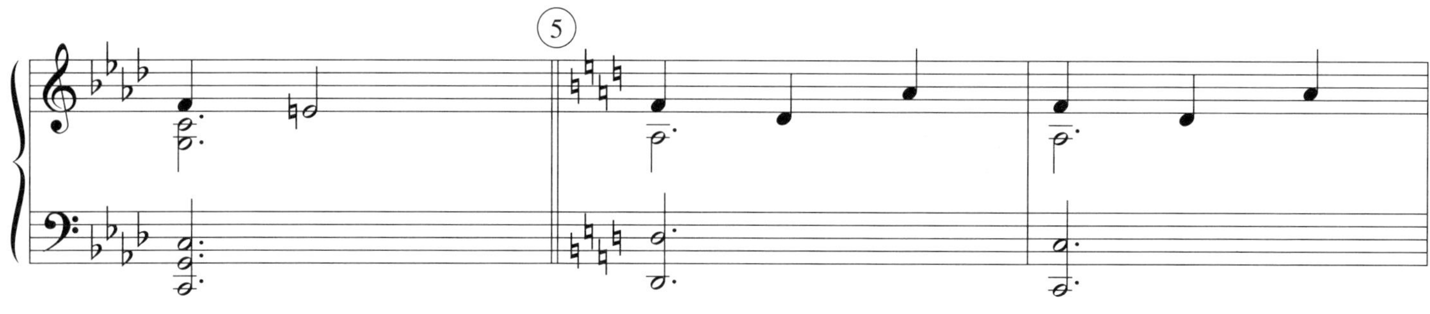

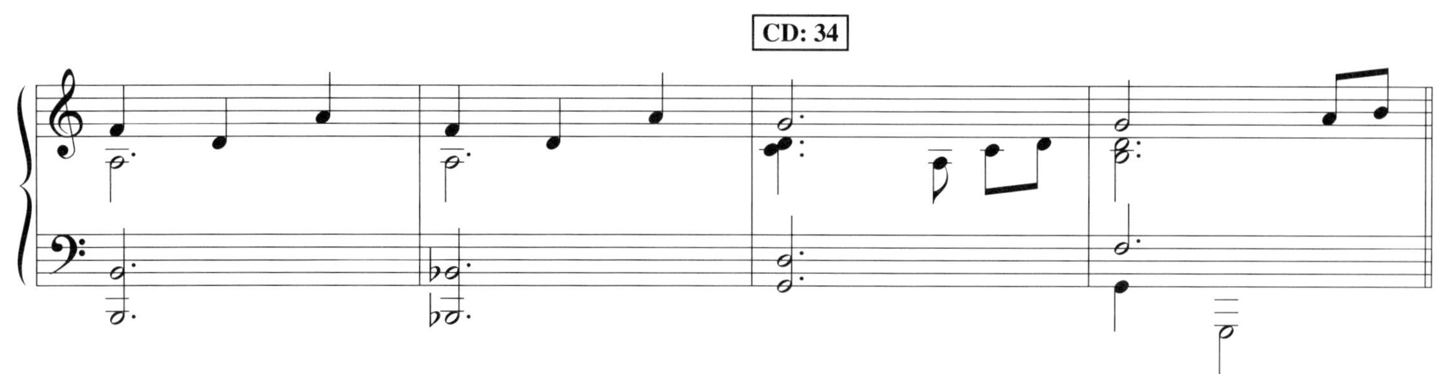

11
Unison
mp
Born is the King, Let prais - es
Unison
mp
11
ring, He is the King of
15
15
Is - ra - el!

Praise to the King

King of Kings
We Bow Down
All Hail, King Jesus

Arranged by Marty Parks

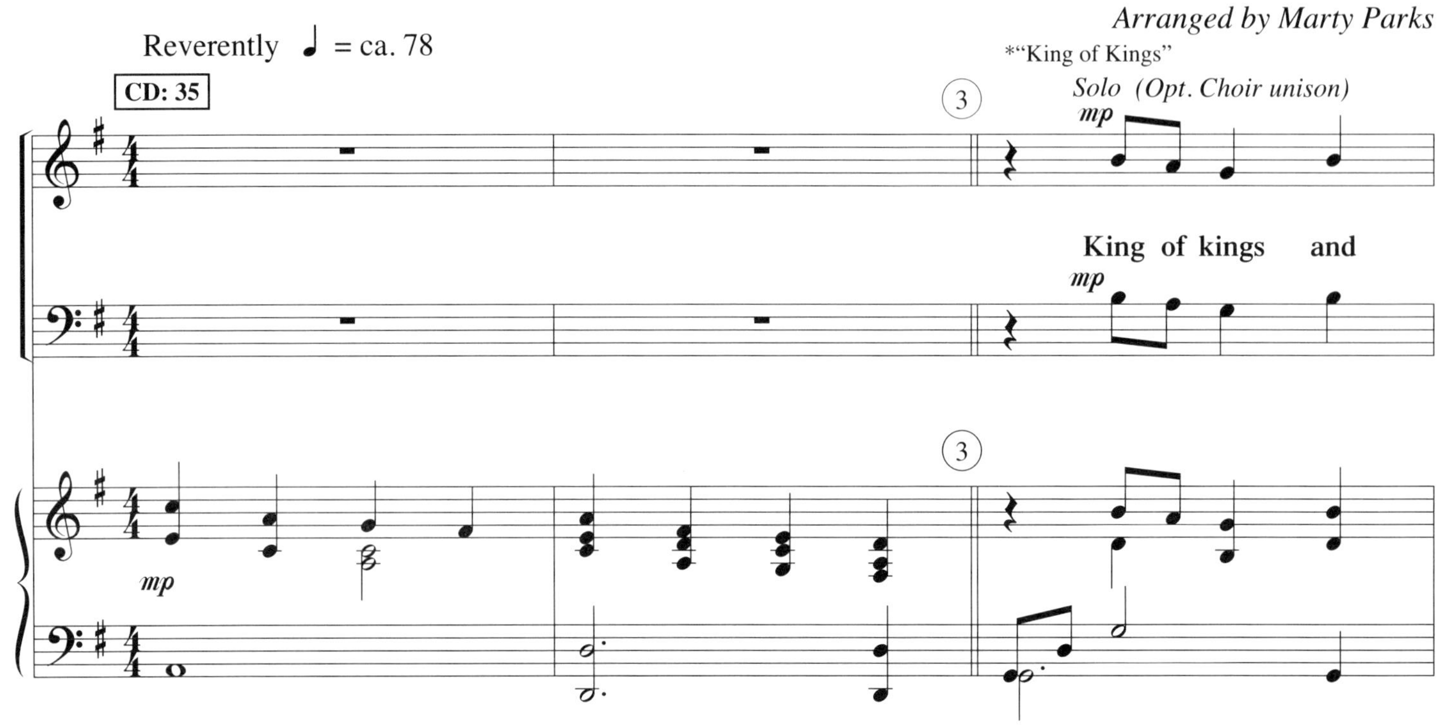

God, the great I Am.
11
Prince of Peace You are, Bright-est Morn - ing
11
Star; Je - sus, I love You, And
15
(,)
(,)
15

CD: 36
Lord, I wor - ship You.
20
Divisi mf
King of kings and Lord, Won-der-ful Coun - sel -
Divisi mf
20
mf
or; Al - might - y God, the great I
24
24

28
Am.
Prince of Peace You are,
28
Bright-est Morn - ing Star;
32
Je - sus, I
32
love You, And Lord, I wor - ship You.
(,)
(,)

*Words and Music by TWILA PARIS. © 1984 by Singspiration Music. (ASCAP) (admin. by Brentwood-Benson Music Publishing Inc.) All rights reserved. Used by permission.

47

King of the land and the sea. You were King of the heav - en be -

47

CD: 38

fore there was time, And King of all kings You will be!

Divisi We bow

51

down and we crown You the King. We bow down and we

We bow down. We bow

51

CD: 39
55
crown You the King. We bow down and we crown You the King.
down. We bow down.
55
59
We bow down and we
King of all kings You will be!
We bow
Divisi
Unison
59
crown You the King. We bow down and we crown You the King. We bow
down. We bow down.

63
down and we crown You the King.
We bow down.
King of all kings You will
Divisi
63
be!
67
King of all kings You will
67
CD: 40
Majestic ♩ = ca. 92
be!

Unison

73 *"All Hail, King Jesus

All hail King Je - sus. All hail Em - man - u - el, King of Kings, Lord of Lords, Bright Morn - ing Star. Through - out

Unison

77

Divisi

*Words and Music by DAVE MOODY.

81

all e - ter - ni - ty, I'll sing His prais - es,

85

CD: 41

And for - ev - er - more I will reign with

Him. Through - out all e - ter - ni -

89

ty, I'll sing His prais - es, And for -

93

ev - er - more I will reign with Him.

ff

All hail! 97 Praise to the King!

NARRATOR: The good news of the Christmas story is this: Christ came into the world to save sinners. By His perfect life and sacrificial death He has redeemed all those who believe and accept His gracious offer. Is it any wonder that all of earth and heaven respond to the birth of Christ with great joy?

Glory to God in the highest! Born is the King!

The First Noel

Reprise

Traditional English Carol
and KEN BIBLE

W. Sandys' *Christmas Carols*
Arranged by Marty Parks

el the an - gel did say Was to
13
cer - tain poor shep - herds in fields as they
13
17
lay–
In fields where they lay
In fields where they
17

21
keep - ing their sheep
On a cold win - ter's
lay keep - ing sheep,
Cold win - ter's
21
CD: 43
night that was so deep.
night that was so deep.
26
Divisi
No - el, No - el, No -
Divisi
26

(,)
30
el,
No - el!
Born is the
(,)
30
King
of
Is - ra - el!
34
CD: 44
Ladies unison
mf
Then

37
Divisi
by the light of a bril - liant
mf
star, Three wise men came from
41
coun - try far.
45
They hum - bly
Unison mf
45

bowed and wor - shipped there, With
49
CD: 45
gold and myrrh and in - cense
49
rare.
f
54
No - el, No -
Divisi
54

(,)
el, No - el, No - el!
(,)
58
Born is the King of Is - ra -
58
CD: 46
62
el!
62

Unison 66

Now let us

Unison

66

Divisi

all with one ac - cord Sing

Divisi

70

prais - es to our Heav - en - ly

70

Unison
74
Divisi
Lord; With shep - herds, kings and
Unison
Divisi
74
78
an - gels come And wor - ship
78
CD: 47
Christ, the Ho - ly One!

83
Optional descant (solo or small group)
f
No - el, No -
No - el, No - el,
83
el,
No - el, No - el!
(,)
No - el, No - el!
(,)

87
Born is the King of Is - ra -
87
el!
91
ff
He is born,
ff
91
ff
Born is the King!
8vb